Howard B. Wigglebottom
Learns to Listen

W9-BVE-137

Written by

Howard Binkow

Illustrated by

Susan F. Cornelison

Written by: Howard Binkow

Illustrated by: Susan F. Cornelison

Book design by: Tobi S. Cunningham

Thunderbolt Publishing
We Do Listen Foundation
www.wedolisten.com

Acknowledgments

This book is the result of a joint creative effort with Sue Cornelison,
who converted what I had to say into a beautifully illustrated story, Ana Rowe, Karen Binkow and Tobi Cunningham.

I wish to acknowledge and thank all those who reviewed the draft copy prior to publication.
The book became much better by incorporating several of their suggestions.

Jodi Allen, Maxine Arno, Dr. Victoria Barnes, Charley Binkow, Martie Rose Binkow, Nancey Silvers Binkow, Sam Binkow,
Kathy Breighner, Julie Cahalan, Professor Jacqueline Edmondson, Ann Faraone, Joan Fenton, Julie Kasen, George Kaufman,
Joan Leader, William Roach, Professor Elizabeth Sulzby, Karma Tensum, Sandy Walor, and the teachers and students at:

Calusa Elementary, Boca Raton, Florida
Coconut Creek Elementary School, Coconut Creek, Florida
John Quincy Adams Elementary, Dallas, Texas
Sherman Oaks Elementary, Sherman Oaks, California
PS 81 and PS 279 Bronx, New York
Interstate 35 Elementary, Truro, Iowa
VAB Highland Oaks Elementary, Miami, Florida
Mrs. Alexander School, Beverly, Massachusetts
Mountain Laurel Waldorf School, New Paltz, New York
Orchard Place, Des Moines, Iowa

Copyright © 2005 by Howard Binkow Living Trust. All rights reserved.
No part of this book may be reproduced, stored in retrieval systems, or transmitted in any form, by any means,
including mechanical, electronic, photocopying, recording or otherwise, without prior written permission of the author.

Second Printing
Printed in China

ISBN: 978-0-9715390-4-4

I have read this book

☐ once

☐ twice

☐ again and again

This book belongs to

_____

Meet Howard B. Wigglebottom.
Howard is always in trouble at school because . . . well,
Howard just doesn't listen.

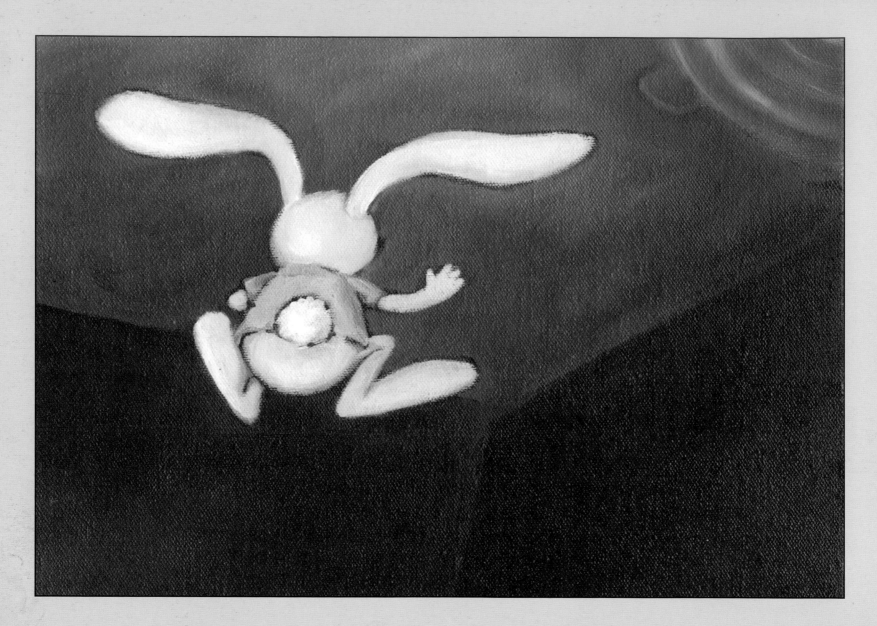

During story time, instead of quietly listening,
Howard bounces around the room.

But Howard doesn't listen.

7

8

But Howard doesn't listen.

9

At lunch time, his friends try to warn him.

But Howard doesn't listen.

After lunch, Howard's friend tries to tell him something important.

But Howard doesn't listen.

On the playground, Howard's teammates try to help him.

But Howard doesn't listen.

In the art room, the teacher reminds the class,
"Kids, try to keep the paint ON your paper."

But Howard doesn't listen.

So the teacher asks him to take a time-out.

He feels sad. Howard does not like being alone and in trouble.
He thinks and thinks about his day.

18

Howard makes up his mind. From that moment on, he will try very hard
to be the best listener he can be.

The next day, Howard DOES listen during story time.

He waits for his turn to talk and then asks
a question about the story.

Howard
gets a
#1 Listener star
because
**Howard is
really
listening.**

While walking home Howard uses both his eyes and ears
to help stay safe. **Howard is really listening.**

When Howard gets home, he listens to his mother.

Howard is really listening.

Awesome ears, Howard!

So Howard gets extra time
to play and have fun.

Howard B. Wigglebottom is really listening . . .

. . . ALMOST all of the time.

HOW TO BE
A BETTER LISTENER

1. Sit quietly.

2. Use both your eyes and your ears to help you listen.

3. Please don't interrupt. Wait your turn to talk.

4. Try your very best to understand the person speaking.

5. Ask questions if you don't understand.

6. Remember rules and directions.

7. Pay attention. That means to be alert and really know what is happening around you.

Listening Discussion Questions

Page 4. ★ What did you learn about listening from Howard B. Wigglebottom?

★ What kind of trouble have you gotten into for <u>not</u> listening? How did it make you feel?

Page 7. ★ How do you think the other students feel about Howard when he is bouncing around and not listening to the teacher?

★ When is it hard for you to sit quietly and listen?

Page 9. ★ How do you think Howard feels when his ears get caught in the fan?

Page 11. ★ Can you think of other times when it's important to use both your eyes and ears to listen?

Page 13. ★ Is Howard doing his best to listen and understand his friend?

★ How do you think Howard's friend feels because she can't finish what she wants to say?

Page 15. ★ Paying attention means being alert and knowing what is happening around you.

★ Was Howard paying attention?

★ What might happen to you if you're not paying attention?

Page 17. ★ Is Howard being respectful to his friend?

Page 18. ★ Do you remember a time when you felt like Howard? How did it make you feel?

Page 19. ★ How do you think the other students felt about Howard before he decided to be a better listener?

★ Do you have any ideas that might help Howard be a better listener?

Page 21. ★ How do you think the other students feel about Howard now that he has decided to be a better listener?

★ Do you wait your turn to talk and then ask questions if you do not understand?

Page 22. ★ When is it easy for you to really listen?

Page 23. ★ Can you think of other times when it is important to follow directions and to use your eyes and ears to keep you safe?

Page 25. ★ Why is it important to be a better listener at home and at school?

Page 27. ★ How do you think Howard feels now that he is a better listener?

Page 29. ★ If you listen better, what might happen to you?

Learn more about Howard's other adventures.

Howard B. Wigglebottom Listens to His Heart

Howard B. Wigglebottom Learns About Bullies

Visit www.wedolisten.com

Print *How to be a Better Listener* from page 30.

Enjoy free games and songs.

You may email the author at
howardb@wedolisten.com

Comments and suggestions are appreciated.